# MARKING TIME

## THE RADIUM GIRLS OF OTTAWA

Thanks!
Heinz Suppan

Heinz-Dietrich Suppan

Marking Time
The Radium Girls of Ottawa

v5.0



Outskirts Press, Inc.
http://www.outskirtspress.com

ISBN: 978-1-4787-6886-9



PRINTED IN THE UNITED STATES OF AMERICA

# Table of Contents

# Introduction

At the turn of the $20^{th}$ Century there was a positive feeling in most of the industrialized nations that a new century would produce an era of miracles that would change mankind. People believed there would be solutions that would address many of the problems they had suffered since the beginning of recorded history.

The development of radium was considered as one of these miracles that would be used to cure many diseases and improve beauty by enhancing newly developed cosmetics, promising a more attractive appearance that became popular in the 1920s.

There were no standards of safety in the early decades of the century. This would create health hazards and alarm people that this miracle would prove to be dangerous and even fatal to those who used these products or worked with radium.

During the First World War radium proved to be successful in being used to paint watch dials so they would be easier to read in the dark trenches.

After the war, the use of radium in the 1920's in the United States and Europe became commercialized. It enhanced the production of pocket and wrist watches, alarm clocks and instrument panels for vehicles and the growing aircraft industry.

In the early 1920's the production of radium dials had spread from the parent companies in the east to the Midwest and to Ottawa, Illinois located in LaSalle County in northern Illinois. The community located about 100 miles southwest of Chicago was blessed with commercial transportation with its location on the Illinois and Fox Rivers and the Illinois & Michigan Canal. Ottawa was also connected to both the Mississippi Valley and Chicago by the Rock Island Railroad.

In the early 1920's Ottawa was a small community of 10,000 inhabitants. There were many factories in Ottawa and even the world's largest cucumber green house. The town was surrounded by a well developed agricultural area. Coal mining was one of the major industries and the presence of silica sand and several glass producing companies created many jobs for the people living in LaSalle County.

When the Radium Dial Company opened a facility in Ottawa to manufacture luminous dials for several watch companies and focused on hiring local women and offered what at that time was considered as fantastic wages for those workers were single or still living at home. With their salaries these dial painters saw their chances to buy the new clothing fashions and products that they would ordinarily not be able to afford.

To be sure, there were conflicts for the women who worked at Radium Dial who made much better salaries than those other women who worked in bakeries, grocery stores or dime stores earning an average of five dollars per week. These tensions became more obvious when the dial painters at Radium Dial were becoming ill and some were dying from the effects of what was later identified as radium poisoning. Many people tended to distance themselves from these women as they became sick and were unable to continue working.

When suspicions developed that perhaps the illnesses of these girls came from working with radium, a lot of effort was made by both many city officials and company supervisors to claim that being exposed to radium was not responsible for the devastating symptoms these girls were suffering. There were even rumors that some of the company officials went so far as to make arrangements with some local doctors and lawyers to avoid providing any help to these workers and their families.

Tests were administered by Radium Dial in the 1920's to determine whether radium was causing the illnesses these women were suffering, and the results of these tests were never revealed.

After several large city newspapers in the east began to investigate why so many women working in radium dial factories were becoming sick and dying, the Chicago press began to cover the events that were unfolding in Ottawa.

Although the Radium Dial Company did not encourage the dial painters to use a technique known as lip-pointing, most of the girls used it. They would put a small camel-hair brush between their lips and pointed the brush with their tongues to paint the hands and numerals on a watch dial with more accuracy. While lip pointing was not required, it was also not discouraged. The supervisors told the workers the radium based paint was safe and even if it was swallowed, it would actually make their cheeks rosy and would enhance their attractiveness.

What caused the illnesses to become more evident were the antics the dial painters did rather than just painting the dials while working. They would often use the excess radium to paint their eyelids, their nostrils, lips, gums and even their ears and fingernails. The workers would then go into darkened areas and blink their eyes, smile and wave their fingers at each other creating eerie green facial features at each other. While it seemed to be a cheap form of entertainment their actions would prove to be toxic and would eventually result in the development of cancer and in most cases, death.

Although the newspapers covered the events that happened at Radium Dial, and many high school and college biology and chemistry classes across the nation discussed the effects of radium and what had happened to these dial painters, no one actually knew where in many cases these stories originated.

Even the city leaders tried to play down these events and avoid discussions fearing it would discourage new industries from locating in Ottawa or more people from moving into the area.

Eventually science would become involved and standards and regulations would be established by state and federal governments to protect workers from exposure to radioactivity.

Laws were eventually passed which would protect workers from an unsafe environment and would give them the authority to pursue legal action.

Another problem for Ottawa developed in 1969 when the rubble and radium from the demolished Ottawa Township High School building was scattered in many areas around the town and surrounding areas resulting in the contamination of soil and also created some suspicions of polluting the ground water. It was not until the 1980's and 1990's the federal Environmental Protection Agency took an active interest in what happened in Ottawa and established a superfund of millions of dollars to clean up several areas which is still an ongoing operation. The contaminated soil was excavated and transported by truck to federally designated areas in Idaho and Washington State.

Ottawa is now a safe place to live but for those who know the history, it is still a difficult subject to address but the story must still be told.

# 1

# Radium: The Miracle Wonder of the 20th Century

While the French scientists Pierre and Marie Curie experimented with uranium, they were successful in 1898 of separating radium from barium and other radioactive compounds which gave off a brilliant green glow. On December 26, 1898 the Curies announced their successful process to the French Academy of Sciences.

*Pierre and Marie Curie*
*Photo courtesy of Wikipedia*

Successful businessmen and brothers, Joseph and James Flannery of Pittsburgh, Pennsylvania were interested in the news about radium that was coming out of Europe. It was heralded as the medical miracle at the beginning of the new 20th Century. Flannery's sister was suffering from cancer and they wanted to do whatever they could to help her. They decided to travel to Europe in order to determine if this "miracle" would save her.

*Joseph and James Flannery*
*Joel Lubenan Collection*

In 1909, the Flannerys went to Europe and were convinced radium would change medicine, just as so many positivists felt the dawn of the new century would change the whole world. Joseph became so fanatical about radium he laced his tomato plants with it, claiming this would revolutionize agricultural production in the United States. He owned a chain of funeral homes in the Pittsburgh area while his brother James operated a vanadium steel company.

In 1911 the Flannery Brothers opened a company known as the Standard Chemical Company in Orange, New Jersey, near Newark to produce and market radium. It was the only successful company in the United States at that time to commercially develop an expensive production system to process radium. The company purchased several mines in Colorado to extract ore that contained uranium.

*The Standard Chemical Company*
*A Brief History of Standard Chemical Company*

The Standard Chemical Company's first commercial product to use radium was called "Undark". It was a mixture of radium and zinc sulfide that was applied to several products using small brushes. Several women who had worked with the tiny brushes to paint designs on pottery and fine quality china were employed by the company to apply their skills to produce these new products.

*Undark Ad*
*Photo courtesy of Wikipedia*

When the United States entered World War I in April, 1917, the U.S. War Department soon realized the problems the soldiers had in trying to read their watches and checking numerical devices in the dark trenches in the French battlefields, to coordinate and organize military strategies. A large government contract was awarded to the Standard Chemical Company by the U.S. War Department to manufacture military watches and other instrument dials using radium paint on the numbers, making it easier for the troops to read in dark areas.

*Military wristwatch - Radium Dial*
*Photo Courtesy of Wikipedia*

More companies were opened by Standard Chemical in Long Island, New York and Waterbury, Connecticut to manufacture luminous dial watches and other instruments to satisfy the demands of the military. These companies became known as the Radio Luminous Material Corporation.

When the war ended and most of the government contracts were cancelled, Standard Chemical established a subdivision of the Radio Luminous Material Corporation to be known as the Radium Dial Company. The only product would be luminous dial watches, alarm clocks and wrist watches with radium painted numerals and clock hands with the radium to be used for military and consumer products.

# 2
# The Charms of Radium and Consumerism

Consumerism gradually increased following several post war strikes demanding better wages, and after the Red Scare which created suspicions towards labor unions and immigrant workers had ended. Radium became the miracle product that had been introduced before the Great War but had been suspended until peace was established. Commercial products that contained radium were promoted not only for watch dials and instrument panels but also for medicinal remedies and cosmetics.

The so called "radium craze" had actually begun as early as 1903 in Europe. After the war, the social media and commercialism began to take control of the demands of American consumers who could afford so many of the new inventions and labor saving devices that flooded the markets in the 1920's.

Consumers who could afford it purchased radios, automobiles, new homes and the latest fashions and styles of clothing. Products began to include radium which also made their sales pitches more desirable.

*Radium Enhanced Products Radium Cakes*

*Tho-Radia Cosmetics*

*Radium Emanation Water*

*Radium Radia*

*Photos Courtesy of Wikipedia*

Newspaper and magazine articles and commercial ads promoted the miracle powers of radium as many commercial products included them in their products. Several items ranging from patent medicines to cosmetics contained radium, claiming they had miraculous healing powers. Radium enhanced products supposedly could cure everything from cancer to high blood pressure. Well known lecturers, poets, even the neighborhood bartenders, barbers and several U.S. governmental agencies were promoting these products. Drinking a concoction of radium according to one advertisement, would cure stomach cancer.

The drink would drench those areas affected from cancer with "liquid sunshine." Another tonic advertised as Radithor, was sold over the counters in U.S. department stores and pharmacies until 1931 when it was finally removed from the market.

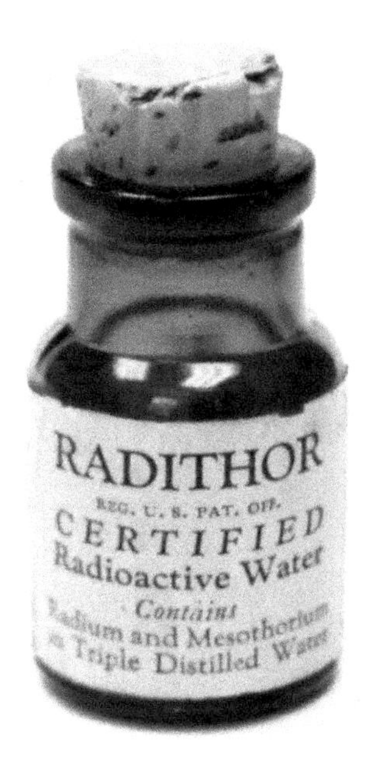


*Radithor*

*Photo Courtesy of Wikipedia*

By 1920, both of the Flannery brothers had died and a board member of the Standard Chemical Company, Joseph A. Kelly, Sr., the son in law of Joseph Flannery, took control of the company. By this time, the Standard Chemical and its subsidiaries had employed more than 1,000 women in Waterbury, Connecticut and Orange, New Jersey who produced more than 4, 300 radium painted dials per day. These women were paid very well for their work.

*Joseph A. Kelly, Sr.*

# 3
# Marking Time with the Radium Dial Painters

As early as 1922 some of these women referred to as "dial painters" were becoming ill with symptoms of radium poisoning. Although no one really knew what this was at the time, the symptoms included anemia, easily fractured bones in the arms and legs, dental problems and the development of tumors. The Radium Dial Company did not officially encourage the lip-pointing process, but this technique was not discouraged.

Lip pointing was a technique the dial painters used when they placed the small bristles of the brushes between their lips and pointed them with their tongues. The small camel hair brushes were used to paint a mixture of water, radium and glue to make a greenish white liquid and was applied to the numbers and hands of the dial. The women were instructed by their supervisors to use lip pointing claiming it would help them produce more dials per day and earn more money. The average dial painter if she was good could complete approximately 250 dials per day. Each worker would use lip- pointing at least six times for each dial they completed.

The company responded to the girls who were becoming ill by claiming radium had nothing to do with their symptoms.

In 1918, the Radium Dial Company opened offices in Chicago to expand its operations into the Midwestern regions. Some of the largest customers in Illinois were the Elgin Watch Company, the Springfield Watch Company and the Westclox Company in LaSalle, Illinois.

The Westclox Company that was established in 1915 asked Radium Dial to open a facility in LaSalle, offering several lucrative contracts to manufacture radium dials for alarm clocks, wrist watches and other types of instruments that used numerical dials. The Radium Dial Company agreed to open a facility in LaSalle to produce luminous watch dials.

*Westclox Building in LaSalle, Illinois*
*Photo by Author*

After a year, Westclox complained that Radium Dial was luring their employees away by offering them better wages.

Officials at Radium Dial decided to look elsewhere to establish a facility to produce luminous dials. They looked in Streator, about 25 miles southeast and in Ottawa, just 20 miles east of LaSalle.

# 4
# Radium Dial Comes to Ottawa

*Map of Illinois and Ottawa*
*Photo Courtesy of Wikipedia*

The old Ottawa Township High School building located at the intersection of Washington and Columbus Streets in Ottawa had been empty since 1916 when the new high school facility was built on Main Street near the Illinois River. Officials of Radium Dial came to Ottawa and selected the old high school building to become the home of a third major facility to produce radium dials. The building was suitable with large windows for optimum light. Several of the old wooden school desks had been left behind, and they could be used by the workers to paint dials.

*Old Ottawa Township High School*
*Courtesy of Wikipedia*

In 1918 Joseph Kelly, the President of the board of directors of the Standard Chemical Company and Radium Dial, came from his offices in New York City to visit Ottawa and inspect the future site of the new location for the Radium Dial Company. In an interview with the local Daily Republican Times newspaper, Kelly said this move would create badly needed jobs and would encourage more industry to locate in the community.

*The Dial Painters at the Radium Dial Facility in Ottawa*
*Courtesy of the Ottawa Scouting and History Museum.*

Radium Dial took out an ad in the newspaper to recruit as many as 70 girls and perhaps there would be more who could earn as much as $18.00 per week, an unheard of salary in Ottawa, where the average salary for a young woman, if she was even able to find work, averaged about $5.00 per week. The ad appealed to many of the girls who had either just completed high school or who had dropped out of school in order to find work to help support themselves and their families. By 1925, there were at least 100 girls working for the Ottawa Radium Dial Company.

Within three years, the Ottawa facility became the largest radium luminous dial production company in the United States.

*The Radium girls at work*
*Photo Courtesy of the Ottawa Scouting and Historical Museum*

The girls were hired for a probationary period to determine whether or not they could learn to paint the dials and meet whatever quotas they were given to be able to satisfy their supervisors. If they did well they were hired to work full time, eight hour shifts six days per week. If they were not able to meet the demands, they were dismissed .

The girls worked on the second and third floors sitting either at school desks or at long tables near large windows where they would prepare the radium mixture and paint dial numbers.

The dial painters were required to wear white smocks over their clothes while they were at work. They would mix the radium powder with water to make the paste to paint the dials. The girls would have to take their smocks home each evening and launder them for the next day's work.

The dial painters were not issued gloves or any kind of protective devices while working with the radium mixture to paint the numerals and hands.

*Radium Dial Painter*
*Photo Courtesy of Wikipedia*

On the main floor, company officials worked with the shipments of radium, remained behind lead screens, wore gloves and masks and used tongs to handle radium containers.

The radium mixture they used had the commercial name "Luna". It was shipped by railroad to Ottawa in barrels and was stored in the basement or in spare rooms of the building.

*Luminous Dial Pocket Watch*
*Photo by Author*

The dial painters were assured by their supervisors and other company officials that Luna was safe. One of their supervisors, who was also the wife of the plant manager, showed them how to properly use lip pointing for their small brushes. She demonstrated her attitude about safety by putting a spatula with radium paste into her mouth.

When one of the girls asked what would happen if they accidentally swallowed some of the paste, the supervisor told her not to worry, that it would make her cheeks rosy and improve her complexion. But despite this, Radium Dial had no official policy that compelled the dial painters to use the lip pointing technique to keep their brushes tapered.

The average dial painter would have to lip point her brush after she painted each numeral. This amounted to roughly 6 times the brush would have to be lip pointed to complete the dial.

# 5

# In the Glow of Radium, Death Lurked in the Shadows

Most of the girls who worked at Radium Dial were in their late 20's. Many of them were unmarried and still lived at home. They were paid well and were able to purchase the latest fashions of clothes, good quality jewelry and high heel shoes. They would often make shopping trips by train or by automobile to Chicago or Peoria. They were also able to contribute money to help their family's finances.

Dial painting often became monotonous and the girls would talk and joke with each other until they were told by their supervisors to stop and continue with their work.

There were occasions when the morning shift was about to end for lunch the girls would empty out the jars that contained the radium. They would often take the remnants of the radium paste and paint their fingernails, ears, nostrils, lips or their teeth and go into a darkened area to smile, blink their eyes, having fun entertaining each other.

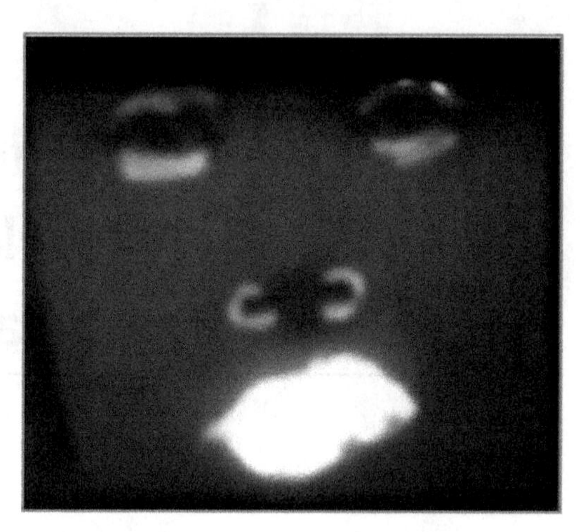

*Dial Painter Enjoys Radium Antics.*
*Photo Courtesy of Wikipedia*

There was another way to entertain their family members or friends. Some of the workers would put some of the radium powder in their handkerchiefs and put them in their purses and brought them home. Later in the evening when it became dark, they would get their friends attention by pretending to sneeze and sprayed the green glowing particles from their handkerchiefs into nearby darkened areas.

By 1925 some of the dial painters in Ottawa were beginning to experience the same symptoms as those who worked in the Orange, New Jersey plant. They were suffering from anemia, fractured bones, dental extractions that would not heal, and tumors that began to form on their jaws and legs.

One of the dial painters was Margaret "Peg" Looney, a quiet, well read redheaded girl. She was the oldest of ten children, two boys and eight girls, of an Irish Catholic family that lived on Columbus Street in a two bedroom house about six blocks north of Radium Dial. She went to work as a dial painter after she graduated from St. Xavier's Academy now known as Marquette Academy. Peg was known to be a practical joker and participated with others to use radium to entertain her friends. After a few months, she began to show the symptoms of radium poisoning. She was tested in 1925 and again in 1928, but the results of these tests were never revealed to Peg or to her family. Her teeth began to fall out and tumors formed on her jaw. Her declining health eventually forced her to resign from Radium Dial. Looney's friends stated her boyfriend Chuck would put the frail girl in a wagon and pull her around the neighborhood because she was too weak to walk to get fresh air or to talk with neighbors. They were planning to be married the following year. On August 14, 1929, just ten days after she resigned from Radial Dial, Peg Looney died at the age of 24.

*Death Lurks Over the Radium Dial Painter*
*Photo Courtesy of Wikipedia*

A company doctor performed an autopsy and listed the cause of her death as diphtheria. He recommended to the family to arrange for an immediate funeral at St. Columba Church to be followed by a prompt burial. The members of the Looney family had doubts about the official report of the autopsy but they were never able to get any information.

In 1978, Looney's remains were exhumed from St. Columba Cemetery in Ottawa and taken to the Argonne National Laboratory located near Naperville for examination.

*Tombstone of Margaret Looney*
*Photo by Author*

A test of Looney's remains by scientists and doctors revealed her bones had more than 1000 times the amount of radium considered as safe levels for human beings. Her remains were encased in a lead casket and returned for reburial.

*Entrance of St. Columba Cemetery*
*Photo by Author*

When some of the workers became ill, they thought that hopefully they would recover, but in most cases their symptoms became so bad they underwent amputations of arms and legs. Often times they became so anemic they could no longer walk or even sit upright.

On June 9, 1928 Joseph Kelly took out a full page ad in an Ottawa newspaper stating that his employees were not suffering from radium poisoning. He claimed their symptoms were the results of typhus or pneumonia. There were rumors that Kelly made deals with some of the local doctors instructing them to comment to the press that many girls were suffering from syphilis. As unmarried Catholic girls living in a small town like Ottawa, this would do irreparable damage to their reputations and to their families who might consider some type of legal action. Kelly hoped these false accusations would persuade the girls and their families not to proceed with any type of legal action against Radium Dial.

No one in the community dared to question the officials at Radium Dial. Many local lawyers and physicians tended to distance themselves from any possible cases involving legal action or damaging their reputations and may have been bribed.

# 6
# The Company Cover up to Avoid Panic

Most of the girls who became sick never took any action for fear of being fired. They liked their salaries and their abilities to make a better living for themselves and their families. In a town like Ottawa, they probably would not have any kind of support from the community because it would hurt the reputation of the town, and people might not want to come here to live or to establish a business.

As more of the girls became ill, the company officials suspected that exposure to radium might have something to do with these illnesses. After tests were administered they felt something should at least be done to make working conditions safer and the managers had a responsibility to inform the workers of what dangers there were. The results of these tests however were never shared with the workers or their families.

Some of the girls and their families went to Chicago to find legal help but due to the lack of sufficient funds litigation was never begun.

In 1924 four radium dial painters who worked for the U.S. Radium Company in Orange, New Jersey became very ill and died under what were described by the local press as "mysterious circumstances".

Several news reporters from New Jersey wanted to get headlines and by lines in local newspapers, and they launched a crusade against the company focusing on how the workers were exposed to such dangerous working conditions. The term "Radium girls" was coined by the reporters during their investigative reporting against the Radium Dial Company and the Radio Luminous Material Company.

The workers eventually won their lawsuit and were awarded $10,000 plus for the rest of their lives, their medical and legal expenses would be covered.

Sven Kjaer, an official with the U.S. Department of Labor Statistics visited radium dial factories in the east and the Ottawa Radium Dial facility in 1925 and said he found little evidence and rejected any theories that radium was harmful to the dial painters.

The supervisors assured the dial painters there was no harm, and once again, they said if some of the radium laced paint was ingested by the women, it would improve their complexions and make them more attractive.

Arthur Roeder, the corporate treasurer of the Radium Luminous Materials Corporation became president of the company. He claimed the problems resulting from the sickness of many of the dial painters were not due to the practices in the factories and that it was merely an attempt to place the blame on the company in order to make them pay. Roeder also was concerned about the negative publicity the company received through various newspapers and the growing concerns of several women's clubs in New Jersey.

In Chicago, Kjaer met with representatives of the Radio Chemical Company and the Radium Dial Company to discuss the growing number of illnesses that were reported in Ottawa. Several employees had been examined regarding the symptoms they showed. Kjaer was told that because Radium Dial was located in a small Midwestern town, it would be difficult to maintain a sufficient work force if the results of the tests were made available. Kjaer was instructed to handle the subject of radium poisoning carefully so as to not cause alarm among the workers unless there were circumstances that would absolutely justify it.

Standard Chemical Company, the parent company, refused to make any comments to the press or to the dial painters because the officials were still not sure that the dial painting created enough dangers to unduly cause alarm among the workers.

In 1925 Kjaer discovered some of the results of Peg Looney's tests while she was still employed at Radium Dial. The results of these tests revealed there may have been enough radium in her body that was highly radioactive and lethal.

At the Radium Dial Company in Pittsburgh, Pennsylvania several dial painters who were working with radium, began to suffer many of the same symptoms, but the company successfully hid any reports of these illnesses until 1928.

Kjaer learned of the cases in Pittsburgh so he suspected after reviewing the situation in Ottawa, that radium could be the cause of these illnesses. He was also concerned about the research that was being conducted by two scientists identified as Charles Viol and William Cameron. They were trying to determine what levels of radioactivity would be considered dangerous and its consequences on anyone who made direct contact with radium.

# 7
# The "Radium Girls" Organize

Several girls at U.S. Radium Materials Corporation filed the first lawsuit which was covered by the press. The dial painters won their case and would receive $10,000 plus $600 per year for the rest of their lives. Additionally, the company would be required to pay all medical and legal expenses.

In 1927 the Radium Dial Company officially took measures to prohibit the practice of lip pointing after so many cases of illnesses erupted in New Jersey and Connecticut that resulted in legal action.

Ella Cruse, a dial painter in Ottawa began to develop similar symptoms after she began losing teeth and tumors began to appear on her body.

*Ella Cruse*
*Photo from Reddick Library*

Another dial painter, Marie Rossiter, who was married and had a son, confronted her supervisor; Rufus Reed. She wanted to know why the results of the tests performed on the girls had not been posted or given to the workers. Mr. Reed responded in a casual manner claiming if the results had been revealed to the workers, "there would be a riot in the place".

*Marie Rossiter*
*Photo from the Reddick Library*

The next day, Ella Cruse filed a petition with the Illinois Industrial Commission for workers compensation after she began to suffer from a facial infection that caused her a great deal of pain.

The Illinois Department of Factory Inspections found that all possible safeguards were in place by 1927 in the Radium Dial facility in Ottawa. The camel hair brushes had been replaced with a glass stylus and the use of the lip pointing technique was no longer permitted.

After some information was published it was determined that there were 31 factories that employed more than 2,000 dial painters who worked with radioactive substances. There were 51 employees at the U.S. Radium plant in New Jersey and six workers at the Waterbury, Connecticut facility, who suffered from symptoms of radium poisoning. There were two employees in Ottawa who were tested, but once again, the results would cause a disruption of their business. They wanted to avoid a panic that might spread among the workers or feared some type of legal action would be taken against the company.

The U.S. Bureau of Labor Statistics recommended the following measures be taken.

1. Advise all workers they should be examined and those who were in ill health, especially from dental problems and anemia should be excluded from the work force.

2. Employees should be examined every two months for radium deposits and blood changes. If they were found and it affected job performance the dial painter should be transferred to other types of work.

3. Dial painters should be educated about the dangers of their work and trained to take precautions. These precautions should include direct contact of the fingers with radium and the lip-pointing of the brushes.

4. All food should be consumed in designated safe areas. Personal hygiene such as hand washing is important and the company must provide proper washing facilities.

5. Ready mixed paint with radium should be used rather than powdered ingredients to minimize the inhalation of radium dust.

6. Well ventilated workspaces to reduce the inhalation of radium dust must be provided. Lead paint containers, lead work-surfaces and well spaced work stations should be installed and used in areas where the dial painters work. where the dial painters work.

# 8
# Just a Fad or Serious Competition?

In 1928 a conference on the uses of radium was held to discuss the reported illnesses of several workers. Those who attended the conference included executives from the radium dial painting companies from New Jersey, Connecticut and Illinois along with representatives from the U.S. Labor and Public Health Departments.

There were also several physicians, and health scientists who had interest in radium poisoning and its affects, but yet no radium dial painters were invited to attend the conference.

Ethelbret Stewart, who headed up the U.S. Bureau of Labor Statistics, raised the issue that the use of radium to paint clock and watch dials was just a passing fad. He questioned whether this so called fad was worth the lives of 13 women and seven men and the serious illnesses of 18 women and five men who were still alive but for how long. Stewart also questioned whether there was sufficient liability in the manufacturing of radium dials to pay for the medical expenses and possible lawsuits that might be initiated by those workers who were suffering from their exposure to radium.

A professor from Purdue University who had close ties with the radium industry argued for the industrial development and the expansion of radium manufacturing over the health of the workers. He commented there was no industry in America that did not have industrial hazards.

This professor said if the luminous dial industry would be shut down because of a hazard, then every major industry in the U.S. could be closed as a result of suspected dangers and could result in massive problems of unemployment among American workers.

Dudley Ingraham, a representative from a major watch company in Connecticut, defended radium's usefulness claiming he had received several letters from bedridden invalids stating the comfort they had received by being able to read luminous dials. Ingraham also said his mother had told him shortly before her death that her alarm clock with the luminous dial had meant so much to her.

When Kjaer visited Ottawa again in 1929 and again in 1934 he realized that little attention at the radium conference had been given to the radium poisoning situation that was becoming worse.

Ella Cruse who suffered from the same symptoms and Margaret Looney's cases were reviewed by Kjaer in 1929. Both of these women had suffered from the same symptoms of radium poisoning.

Cruse had suffered from degenerating bones in her jaw and Looney had died from what an official autopsy report said was diphtheria and complications of pneumonia. The Looney family continued to reject the results of the autopsy that was conducted on Margaret "Peg" Looney.

Cruse had worked at Radium Dial for four years. More than ten years after she left the company, Cruse died in 1931 at the age of 30. An autopsy revealed an osteogenic sarcoma springing from the periostuem ascending and descending on the left of the pubic bone.

The Cruse family accepted $250 as a settlement from the Radium Dial Company and this action was approved by the Illinois Industrial Commission. Ella Cruse had originally sued for $3,750.

Looney's sister said her family had tried to receive compensation but never received a satisfactory settlement.

# 9
# The Doomed Legions of Ottawa

In 1934 seven Ottawa dial painters referred to by the Chicago newspapers as the "Society of the Living Dead" were the first to initiate legal action against the Ottawa Radium Dial Company. They had a problem finding a lawyer who would represent them. It was difficult for the dial painters to raise the funds needed to pay for such action. Those women were identified as Helen Munch, Marie Rossiter, Marguerite Glacinski, Olive Witt, Frances O'Connell, Maxine Smith and Catherine Wolfe Donohue.

*The Society of the Living Dead*
*Photo from the Reddick Library*

The Laborers Union Local 393 in nearby Marseilles, Illinois claimed the workers were not represented by any union. Officials of the union claimed of the 100 women who worked at the Ottawa Radium Dial Company 70 of the workers had developed cancer and died. If any of the workers attempted to lodge a complaint they would be fired. The union raised more than $7,000.00 to help the women with legal expenses.

Catherine Wolfe was a radium dial painter who had worked at Radium Dial for several years. She went to work when she was 19 years old. While she was employed, she married Thomas Donohue who was employed at the Libbey Owens Ford Glass factory in Naplate, a suburb of Ottawa. They had two children, Tom and Mary Jane. The children attended Marquette Grade and High School.

*Catherine Donohue*
*Photo from the Reddick Library Ottawa, Illinois*

The Donohue family lived on Superior Street in Ottawa, about five and a half blocks east of the Radium Dial Company.

Charlotte Purcell also started to work at Radium Dial in 1922 when she was 16 years old. By 1934 Mrs. Donohue and Purcell not only worked together but also became friends. Their families often attended family picnics and went together to many of the city and church's social events.

In 1931, Catherine suffered from pain in her left hip and was dismissed from her job. Her supervisor told her that her noticeable limping caused other workers to talk and that it would be in the best interest of the company to remove her from the work force at Radium Dial.

Charlotte Purcell developed cancer in her left arm and it had to be amputated.

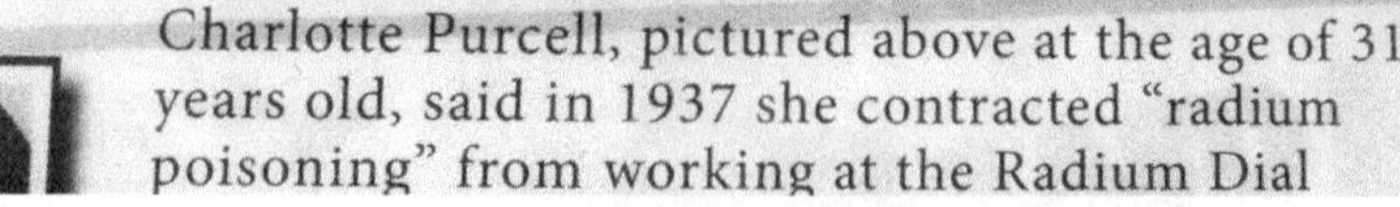

Charlotte Purcell, pictured above at the age of 31 years old, said in 1937 she contracted "radium poisoning" from working at the Radium Dial

*Charlotte Purcell*

*Photo from the Reddick Library*

In April, 1934, Purcell organized a group of nine dial painters at Radium Dial to meet with a physician identified as Doctor Loffler, who was conducting an informal clinic at a local Ottawa hotel. Doctor Loffler agreed to examine the women and his diagnosis revealed they were all suffering from some form radium poisoning.

Using the results of these examinations by a qualified physician, the nine women contacted a lawyer identified as Leonard Grossman from Chicago. He agreed to accept their case and initiated action to file a lawsuit against Radium Dial using the law under the Illinois workers compensation and occupation disease laws. Acting on the advice of the lawyer, Purcell and Donohue went to their supervisor, Rufus Reed and informed him of the illnesses they had developed while they worked at Radium Dial. They said they were filing a lawsuit to receive compensation and medical treatment. Reed told the women there was nothing wrong with them that had resulted from working at Radium Dial. He further denied any evidence of radium poisoning.

Catherine Donohue's husband Tom, who was known for his quick temper, went to Radium Dial to talk with his wife's supervisor, Rufus Reed.

Donohue said his wife and Charlotte Purcell were very sick and he believed his wife's illness was caused by radium that was being used to paint the luminous dials. Reed once again insisted there was no such thing as radium poisoning and that the women were suffering from other types of illnesses not connected with exposure to the radium laced paint.

Donohue then demanded to see the results of the tests that were given to the dial painters in 1925. He also wanted to know the names of the doctors who performed these tests. Donohue told Reed he just wanted to know what the truth was and what made these women and in particular, his wife Catherine, and Charlotte Purcell so sick. Reed refused to release any information and a fight broke out between Donohue and Reed. The local police were summoned to the Radium Dial facility to escort Mr. Donohue from the premises.

In 1934, another dial painter identified as Inez Vallet joined with the nine women to file a lawsuit against the Radium Dial Company. The women asked for $50,000 alleging Radium Dial was in violation of the Occupational Disease Act that required the use of reasonable and approved devices, and the means and methods for the prevention of occupational diseases.

The dial painters found an ally with Reuben Soderstrom of Streator, Illinois. He was president of the Illinois Federation of Labor and he specialized in the obscure occupational diseases laws. As a result of the violation of these occupational diseases these women were suffering from the symptoms of radium poisoning. Soderstrom could give these women the opportunity to take legal action against Radium Dial. The tests that were conducted in 1925 and in 1928 on the dial painters and the results were never posted nor were they released to the workers or their families.

In 1935, Vallet's case came before the Illinois State Supreme Court because a challenge that was made by the lawyers of Radium Dial to question the constitutionality of the Occupational Disease Act. The lawyers argued the law was vague and failed to establish intelligible standards of duty and therefore, violated the due process clauses of the state and federal constitutions. The law permitted inspections to determine just what devices, means and methods employers were required to use, and this law conferred legislative powers on an administrative agency. The Illinois State Supreme Court agreed with the attorneys for Radium Dial that the law was too vague and therefore all of the lawsuits filed by the Ottawa dial painters were dismissed.

Shortly after these cases were dismissed by the State Supreme Court the Illinois General Assembly quickly passed a new law known as the Occupational Disease Act. It was signed into law in March 1936 by Governor Henry Horner while he was in Chicago. This law attempted to be more precise and like the previous law made all industrial diseases and injuries compensable.

*Illinois Governor Henry Horner*
*Photo Courtesy of Wikipedia*

Catherine Donohue, Charlotte Purcell and 13 radium dial painters refiled their lawsuits for compensation under this new law. Inez Vallet, who had originally filed the law suit, died in February just a month before the new occupational disease act was signed into law. According to the symptoms suffered by Ms.Vallet, she had a tooth pulled and the extraction wound did not heal. She also suffered a tumor on her jaw and suffered from a painful limp before she died.

In 1938, the Illinois Industrial Commission began to hold hearings in Chicago on the complaints filed by the Ottawa dial painters. By the time these hearings convened, the illness suffered by Catherine Donohue had become so bad she could barely walk. She only weighed 71 pounds. Her brother in law claimed "she was full of radium and was dying by the inches".

Catherine's husband said he was nearly bankrupt from purchasing so many medications to relieve his wife's pain. Catherine's medical expenses amounted to more than $2,500. Her husband said he had to take out a mortgage on their home at 520 E. Superior Street in order to help cover expenses.

Due to the severe pain Catherine was suffering, it was agreed by court officials to conduct the hearings in the Donohue home while Catherine remained in bed.

The newspapers in Chicago and many other major cities spared no effort using sensationalistic headlines such as "The Doomed Legions of Ottawa", "Their Days are Numbered" and "Ottawa's Living Dead" recounted the lurid details that were brought out in the hearings about the symptoms the dial painters were suffering.

OTTAWA'S DOOMED WOMEN

Ottawa, Ill., March 17.—There's a group of women, dead and ...ving, that Illinois' new occupational disease law can't help.

They're the victims of the dread radium poisoning, contracted ...rom employment at the Radium Dial Co., here. Their battle for ...ome monetary remu...ration for the physi...al torture, loss of ...mbs and slow, painful ...eath, ended 10 months ...go with the scrapping ...f Illinois' old occupa...tional disease law, de...clared unconstitutional ...y the state Supreme ...ourt.

Gov. Horner signed the new ...aw in Chicago last night. It ...ets up rates of compensation ...or victims of occupational ...iseases, where the old was "vague and indefinite."

No amount of money could ...ave the life of a radium poi...on victim, but it could help to ...ake her remaining years of ...e comfortable. No law could ...islate it out of her system

INDUSTRIAL MARTYR

10 WOMEN DIE, 15 OTHERS ARE ILL AT OTTAWA

(Continued from page 1)

from cancer, tumor, pneumonia, hemorrhage and other ailments. Others, still young, many of them mothers, hobble about their homes with locked hips, swollen limbs, their frames wracked with pain, an amputated arm, distorted faces.

DIE WITHOUT "CAUSE"

Young girls, with strangely similar symptoms, have been dying off for 13 years in Ottawa, without any official comment or investigation. All had been employed by the radium company to paint the dials of watches and clocks and other gadgets with luminous paint. All were taught to "point" their paint brushes with their mouths.

The story of Ottawa's Radium Dial Co. closely parallels that of the much-publicized victims of U. S. Radium Corp. of Orange, N. J., except that the latter eventually won their court fight.

In fact, when the story of the ...

*Headlines of Ottawa's Doomed Women*

*Photo from the Reddick Library*

During the trial other workers appeared to give testimony about the deplorable conditions of the Ottawa Radium Dial facility. Some of the questionable practices began to surface about the physical exams that were given in 1925 and 1928 and that the results of these tests were never given to the workers or to their families.

An article appeared in the Peoria Journal Star reporting that when the workers complained of illnesses and symptoms of tumors, dental problems and anemia company doctors said these symptoms were caused by typhus, pneumonia or by syphilis.

Marie Rossiter mentioned that when she worked at Radium Dial, there were ten girls working in her area, and within a few years, four of them were dead. Mrs. Rossiter said she was scared to death that she would be next and she wanted to live for her son, Bill. She said that she and other dial painters would paint their eyelids, teeth and gums, lips and fingernails with radium residue and go into darkened areas to blink their eyes, smile or make faces and wave their radium drenched fingers to entertain each other.

*Marie Rossiter*
*Courtesy of the Reddick Library Ottawa, Il.*

Mrs. Rossiter developed large tumors on her legs and one of her legs had to be amputated. She was featured in the documentary film, Radium City that was produced in 1987. It was about the radioactivity that still existed in Ottawa and what measures had been taken to clean up several areas. She died in 1993 and is buried in St. Columba Cemetery.

*Tombstone of Marie Rossiter*
*Photo by Author*

# 10

# Drama in the Donohue Home

On February 10, 1938 twelve former dial painters at Radium Dial appeared before George C. Maxwell, arbitrator of the Illinois Industrial Commission, claiming their illnesses were the results of working with radium to paint the watch dials.

Catherine Wolfe Donohue was the first dial painter to have her case settled by the State Industrial Commission. Her situation proved to be the test case in this hearing. Mrs. Donohue testified she was employed from 1922 to 1931 as a dial painter at Radium Dial. She said she had been a healthy active woman and now, she had become an invalid weighing nearly 70 pounds. She said it had become impossible for her to kneel during mass at St. Columba Church and that her teeth were falling out. She also was suffering from a tumor on her hip that caused her to walk with a noticeable limp.

*Catherine Donohue with daughter*
*Photo from Reddick Library*

During the hearing, Attorney Grossman who had been retained to represent the dial painters, called Dr. Walter Dollisch to testify regarding the physical condition of Mrs. Donohue. Dr. Dollisch was a former dentist who was now a practicing surgeon. Attorney Grossman asked Dr. Dollisch in his professional opinion whether Mrs. Donohue's condition would result in "certain death". Before Dr. Dollisch was able to respond Mrs. Donohue slumped into a chair and began to sob.

She had to be carried out her room. Her husband also broke down and cried after watching his wife being removed from the hearing after she was told she was dying from radium poisoning.

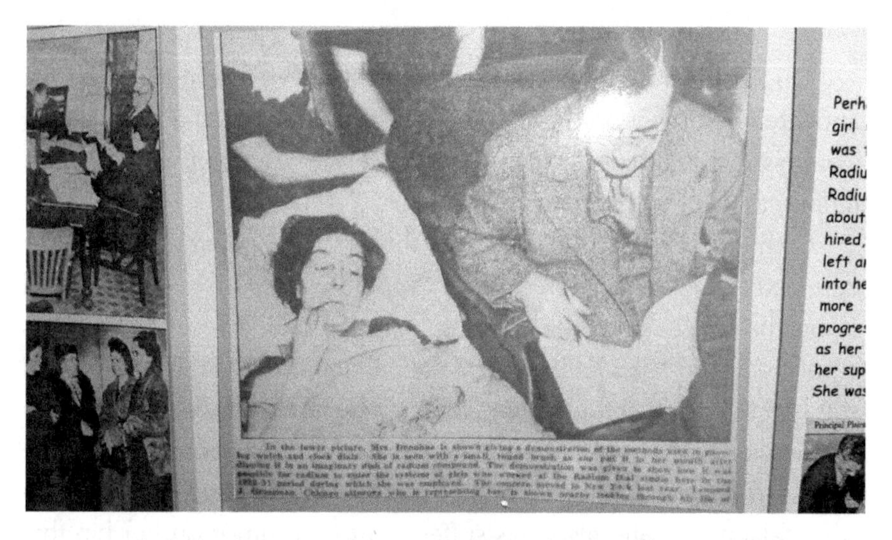

*Catherine Donohue demonstrates the technique of lip pointing*
*Photo courtesy of the Ottawa Scouting and Historical Museum*

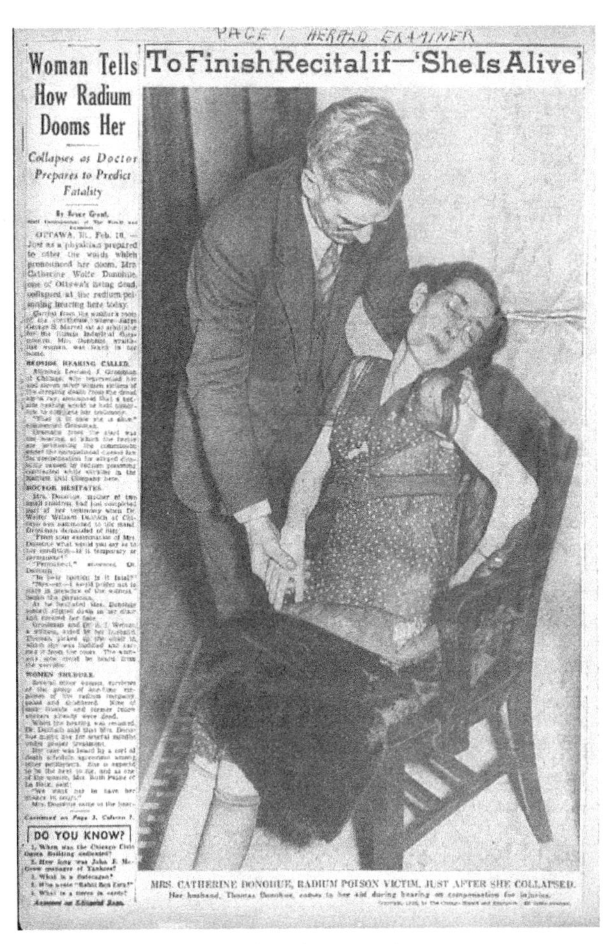

PAGE 1 HERALD EXAMINER

# Woman Tells How Radium Dooms Her

## To Finish Recital if—'She Is Alive'

*Collapses as Doctor Prepares to Predict Fatality*

OTTAWA, Ill., Feb. 10.—Just as a physician prepared to utter the words which pronounced her doom, Mrs. Catherine Wolfe Donohue, one of Ottawa's living dead, collapsed at the radium poisoning hearing here today.

DO YOU KNOW?

MRS. CATHERINE DONOHUE, RADIUM POISON VICTIM, JUST AFTER SHE COLLAPSED.
Her husband, Thomas Donohue, comes to her aid during hearing on compensation for injuries.

*Catherine Donohue fainting after testimony*

*Photo from Catherine Donohue Collection Northwestern University*

Hearings and legal processes were also conducted in New Jersey and in Pennsylvania. Several of the dial painters had died or had become very ill with the same symptoms the Ottawa dial painters had experienced. It was in these areas that the local newspapers began using the term "Radium Girls of Ottawa".

In April 1938 Catherine Donohue was awarded $3,320 for medical expenses and $2,395 for compensation and an annual pension of $378 for the rest of her life.

EPUBLICAN-TIMES

FINAL EDITIO

REORGANIZATION FOES' HOPE OF VICTORY WANES

Radium Dial Test Case Won By Mrs. Donohu

COMPENSATION IS AWARDED B STATE BOA

*Headline Catherine Donohue Wins Case*
*Photo from the Reddick Library*

Catherine Donohue died in July, 1938 at the age of 35 before she received any of the compensation she had won in court. The day after her death, the legal team from the Radium Dial Company went into action to file an appeal of the award that was given to the Donohue family.

*Grave Catherine Donohue*
*Photo by Author*

The State ordered that before an appeal could be made, Radium Dial would have to post a bond. The reason for this was the company was self insured and since 1931 the potential for compensation for the lawsuits that were filed made it impossible for Radium Dial to purchase compensation insurance. Another reason for posting the bond was that Radium Dial had closed their offices in Chicago and was no longer doing business under the name of Radium Dial in Illinois.

In 1937, the U.S. Radium Company decided to close its Ottawa facility after more citizens and the newspapers began to side with the dial painters were angered by the resistance the company demonstrated to provide any help for the worker.

Most of the residents in Ottawa thought the problem was over and a sense of normalcy would return.

After the old Ottawa High School building was vacated, a meat packing business moved into the basement area and provided fresh meat to local customers, restaurants and grocery stores. Later, the Farmers Co op moved into the building. In 1969, the building was demolished at a cost of $16,000.

# 11
# The City that Failed to See the Light

Many residents in Ottawa were looking for mementos from the school and took away desks, tables, light fixtures and bricks from the building. Some of the items were taken into their homes and many of the bricks were used in the construction of new homes or repairs to many of the brick streets.

Most of the buildings' remains were used for landfill in several areas around Ottawa including an area adjacent to the Marquette High School athletic field on the Fox River. The radioactivity in this rubble would remain hot for the next 40 years.

*Marquette High School Academy Athletic Field*
*Photo by Author*

Some of the rubble was deposited near Buffalo Rock State Park about six miles west of Ottawa. Many hunters provided photos of deer they had shot in that area that had large tumors.

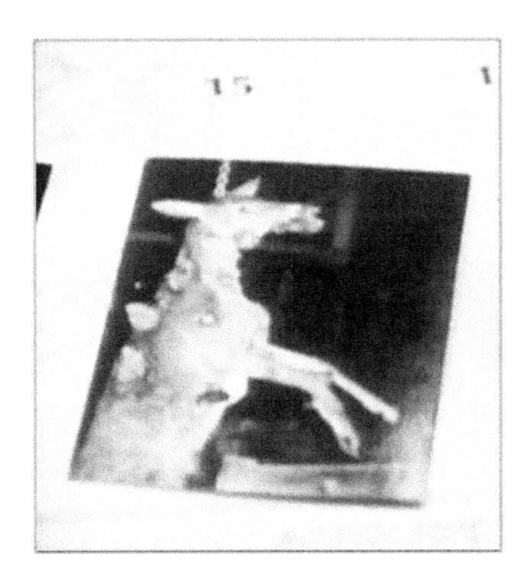

*Deer with tumors*
*Photo courtesy of Greenroad Blogspot*

The workers deposited a lot of the contaminated rubble near Canal Road that runs along the Illinois & Michigan Canal between Ottawa and Marseilles. In the 1970's a family purchased a home near this area. Their son who played outside near the area, became ill and after an examination, it was determined he had been exposed to high amounts of radioactivity. He had to have a large section of his liver removed. He recovered from the surgery and regained his health.

# 12

# A New Radium Facility Opened in Ottawa

In June 1934 just six weeks after the Radium Dial Company closed its offices at the old Ottawa High School, U.S. Radium President Joseph Kelly made plans to open another radium production company in Ottawa under a different name: Luminous Processes Corporation. The plant was located at Fulton and Jefferson Streets, about six blocks from the old Radium Dial Company. The two story yellow brick building would be used to continue making radium dials and other instruments. One of the largest contracts it received was from the Westclox Company.

*Luminous Processing Inc. Building*
*Photo courtesy of the Ottawa Scouting and Historical Museum*

Some of the dial painters at Radium Dial were invited to a dinner and were encouraged to come to work at Luminous Processes Inc. They were promised better wages and safer working conditions.

There was another story that circulated about the establishment of the Luminous Processes Corp. Joseph Kelly Sr. who had served as president of Radium Dial for more than 20 years, was accused by some of the board members of taking measures to cover up the results of the testing of the employees and the negative publicity of the newspapers about the "Radium girls". He was about to be ousted by the board of directors of the Radium Dial Company.

There were also reports that began to circulate that focused on Kelly who had seen a growing number of lawsuits and governmental investigations by state and local health officials. Kelly decided to have his son, Joseph A. Kelly, Jr. help him to establish Luminous Processes, Inc.

The new company advertised for workers and with it being the depths of the Great Depression, many who were desperate for work applied and were hired. The girls were told the workplace was safe and they would not be using the lip-pointing process. It is true that most of the workers didn't experience the same illnesses as those who worked at Radium Dial, but the symptoms resembled those of radium poisoning.

When Radium Dial closed down its operations in the old Ottawa High School building, many of the dial painters went to work at Luminous Processes Inc.

After Luminous Processes took over the Radium Dial operation, the Illinois Insurance Commission demanded Radium Dial to post a $10,000 bond in order to proceed with an appeal made by the lawyers of Radium Dial in the Donohue case. Lawyers for the Radium Dial Company responded by claiming the company had only $22,000 in assets. Radium Dial challenged the requirement to post the bond but lost in court and had to agree to follow the decision of the State of Illinois Insurance Commission.

Radium Dial lawyers went to work to challenge the award made to the Donohue family but lost seven consecutive appeals. In 1939 an appeal was made to the U.S. Supreme Court but the court refused to hear the case.

The Donohue award was for $5,700 and it was to be was paid from the bond that was posted. The remainder of the bond was paid to the rest of the women who joined together to file suit against Radium Dial. Charlotte Purcell received only $300. Three of the women had withdrawn their lawsuits after the lawyers who had been retained by the Radium Dial Company continued to file appeals.

# 13
# Ottawa Patriotism and Federal Standards

When the U.S. entered World War II in December 1941 President Franklin D. Roosevelt and scientist Albert Einstein met with Joseph Kelly who owned Luminous Processing and other factories in the east that used radium. Kelly converted Luminous Processes to work with reprocessed radium to develop polonium, a key element used in the development of the atomic bomb. In Ottawa, several of the women claimed they were not sure what they were working on, but they were told their work was important for the war effort and it was their chance to demonstrate their patriotism for the United States.

During the war, luminous dials were in high demand for military equipment and instrument panels in aircraft. The number of companies across the U.S. that manufactured luminous dials expanded to meet the demands of war production quotas.

The government was concerned about the health of the workers in these companies, but only because of the quotas that had to be met. The government conducted investigations into the safety and health of those workers in the defense industries and that included the production of radium dials.

Until 1941, there were no official guidelines that had been established for the standards of radiation exposure. When large scale production for military equipment began it was determined that safe level of standards in the production of radium dials needed to be established.

An advisory committee on x-ray and radium production invited doctors, industrial hygienists, radium industry officials and a naval officer from the National Bureau of Standards to establish what they would consider as safe levels of radium exposure by the workers.

These levels of tolerance established by this committee were only recommendations that would be considered as safety codes to be adopted by the state.

During the war, the maximum amount of radium ingested by the workers often exceeded the levels of tolerance established by the committee.

In Illinois, two employees of the Division of Industrial Hygiene under the Department of Public Health published a review of information they had collected as a part of a nationwide study conducted by the U.S. Department of Public Health.

The data revealed there were six luminous dial plants operating in Illinois and a seventh plant was developed to assemble the instruments that used radium dials.

The report further stated that 36 workers were examined for radium by exhaling to measure any presence of radium in their breath. About half of those workers who were tested showed more than the recommended tolerance levels in their breath which also included the presence of radon. The greatest number of those workers who were tested came from Plant E. The plant identified in their report as Plant E was Luminous Processes Inc. in Ottawa. There were four workers who had previously worked at Radium Dial.

Many of the employees at Luminous Processes had worked with radium from 16 to 20 years. About half of the employees who were tested exceeded the recommended tolerance levels for exposure to radium.

Many said that the dial painting companies in Illinois were safe and it was the negative publicity that focused on the suffering and deaths of the workers who painted the radium dials in the 1920's following World War I that made many think that dial painting was a dangerous occupation for women. The report also mentioned that of the seven Illinois plants that worked with luminous dials, only two of them did not exceed the tolerance levels for radon.

By the end of the war, Kelly had become a multi-millionaire but most of the workers in Ottawa were concerned about themselves and glad they still had a job. Some of the married women had husbands who returned from military service and could not find work, so the women applied at Luminous Processes for a job. They were earning an average of 50 cents to $1.00 per hour.

There was a rule that when the workers left the building for a lunch break, they would have to pass under a black light that would reflect any radioactive material on their hands. They did not wear gloves and it was difficult and often painful to scrub the radium residue from their hands.

The company also produced gauges for commercial and military aircraft and continued to make radium dials for the Westclox Company.

# 14
# Government Intervention and Regulations

The Ottawa plant became a target for discussion after high levels of radium had been detected. An investigation revealed there were no ventilated tables, but some hygienists said that with the windows open in the summer months, the air was tested and it was recorded at a tolerant level and therefore, ventilated work tables would not be necessary.

The workers would be able to work under safe conditions without the need to purchase the expensive ventilation equipment. These hygienists probably never considered what it would be like during the autumn and winter months when the windows were closed.

A study made by the State Department of Health claiming the only danger seemed to be the poor work habits of the dial painters who would get the radium paint on their hands and then touch their mouths with their contaminated hands. To prevent these kinds of incidents, the officials at Luminous Processes were told not to hire women who bit their nails or those who had a habit of wiping their mouths with their hands. Jewelry would not be worn at work and the women would be required to clip their fingernails short to avoid collecting radium dust.

The workers would also wear scarves over their hair and smocks to cover their street clothing. Many of the employers were skeptical about these suggested requirements fearing they would be too difficult to enforce. Proper hand washing would be the easiest regulation for the company to demand of its workers.

The Illinois study claimed the tolerance levels were too low and too expensive to meet, and that the women who worked in these plants with radium were at fault due to their poor work habits.

The dial painters were never informed about the dangers of working with radium. If the companies could blame the workers because of poor work habits, for their problems, the companies would not feel the need to provide proper training or education or be required to purchase expensive equipment to be installed at Luminous Processes Inc.

Pearl Schott, one of the original dial painters, said it was impossible to work at Luminous Processes without getting some of the radium dust on her body. She said she would wake up in the middle of the night and looked into her bedroom mirror to see a green glow coming from her hair. She suffered from dental problems, anemia and gastrointestinal bleeding which were symptoms of radium poisoning.

When an official from the U.S. Radium Company came to Ottawa, Pearl asked him about her symptoms and the official replied that several people suffered from similar symptoms but radium had nothing to do with her illness. The company official attempted to calm her by claiming there was no harm.

Another dial painter, Eleanor Eichelkraut said the girls would sit at long tables talking and joking while painting the dials, not having any idea what danger lurked in their presence.

# 15
# Scientific Investigations of the Ottawa Dial Painters

In 1948, the Argonne National Laboratory was opened and one of its first projects was to contact those radium dial painters who were still alive and have them come to the laboratory for examinations. These sessions would last for an hour and the patients would have to sit in a barber style chair with their arms outstretched on the frame of the chair and be X-rayed. These people were asked to travel twice each year to the Argonne Laboratory for the examinations.

With the permission of the Donohue family, Catherine Wolfe Donohue's remains were exhumed from St. Columba Cemetery. The caretaker of the cemetery Wayne Wiesbrock, mentioned the men who arrived from Argonne came first in a station wagon to collect the body. They had to return with a truck after they learned Mrs. Donohue's body was in a  sealed lead casket that was encased in cement. When Mrs. Donohue's body was exhumed it had a glass lid. Wiesbrock said he could see through the glass and could observe a rosary still in her hand. He said he could also see her dress and shoes. The total weight of the casket was in excess of 2,400 pounds. The concrete encasement had to be cracked open in order free the casket from its vault and to bring the remains to the laboratory for examination. Mrs. Donohue's remains were placed in a body bag and transported to the Argonne Laboratory to be tested for radium deposits that remained in her body.

The examination revealed a large tumor on the hip area that had caused her to limp while she was still employed at Radium Dial. The tests also showed there was enough radioactivity in her bones that would take more than 3,200 years to completely dissipate.

By 1968 the Argonne National Laboratory solicited more than 4,600 workers who had been exposed to radium. Many permitted Argonne to use their bodies to establish standards for nuclear exposure standards.

The workers were never compensated for their participation in these examinations nor were they ever informed of the results.

From Ottawa, 205 workers who had been employed at Radium Dial Company and Luminous Processes Inc. volunteered to be examined. More than 80 percent of those who were examined had radium exposure concerns. It was reported more than 50 of the workers had serious radium cancer related symptoms. Many of those volunteers died before the study ended in the 1990's.

The families of workers who had already died received letters from Argonne requesting permission to exhume the bodies and have them brought to the labs for examinations and to donate the bodies to science.

In 1957, the State of Illinois was charged by the federal government with the enforcement of their regulations of radium.

It was not until 1975 that the State Department of Public Health had the necessary authority to establish regulations to control the safe handling of radium.

About the same time, Luminous Processes switched from using radium in its luminous paints to tritium, a radioactive form of hydrogen. Tritium unlike radium was not regulated by the State but only by the federal government and the Nuclear Regulatory Commission (NRC).

On inspection of Luminous Processes in Ottawa by officials from the NRC, they found the radiation level of the plant 1,666 times greater than that the Commission's allowable levels. The NRC instructed the officials at Luminous Processes to correct the situation. After three more visits by the NRC in 1976 the levels were not significantly reduced and the commission fined Luminous Processes $3,250.00.

# 16
# The End of Radium Production and Clean Up

Two more inspections by the NRC in 1977 and 1978 revealed no major improvements were made and the commission suspended the license of Luminous Processes inc. with the intention to revoke the license if improvements were not made to significantly reduce the levels of radioactivity.

Luminous Processes Inc. in Ottawa was officially closed by the state of Illinois in 1978 as a result of repeated health and safety violations.

The federal government ordered Luminous Processes to clean up the plant and remove all contamination. The company donated some desks to a local Catholic elementary school, but they were returned when it was determined these tables and desks had high levels of radioactivity.

After Luminous Processes closed its doors in Ottawa, the windows of the building were boarded up and a chain link fence was placed around the designated contaminated area.

The building was left standing for the next seven years. Someone using black spray paint painted on the south side of the building "Dial Luminous for Death".

By 1980 ten women who had worked at Luminous Processes experienced high rates of tumors and breast cancer. There were 64 reported deaths among the radium dial painters who had worked at the plant since the 1960's. From 1964 to 1975, 28 of these dial painters had died from cancer or related illnesses.

During the next two and a half years, Luminous Processes officials made promises to clean up the building and its surroundings, however they backed off eventually claiming it would be too expensive. The circuit court of LaSalle County ordered Luminous Processes to clean up the area but once again, the company claimed it lacked the necessary funds.

Luminous Processes attempted to avoid financial responsibility by shifting some of its corporate assets to other holdings like Radium Dial had done in the 1930's.

The State of Illinois brought Luminous Processes, Inc and the Radium Chemical Company into court claiming these companies did have sufficient assets to clean up the site. The State prosecutors agreed to settle out of court for $62,000 which was as much as they would be able to get.

For several years, some of the local government officials claimed there was nothing wrong with the building. James Thomas, a former barber who had served as the Mayor for 20 years claimed the building was safe.

Many concerned citizens made several attempts to bring up the issues of contamination and excess levels of radioactivity at council meetings. Government officials from Springfield addressed a citizens' group about the removal of the vacated Luminous Processes building.

Mayor Thomas had the police to stand by during the meeting fearing there might be problems. The meeting was held without incident but it was only partially informative. More questions were raised than were answered.

Mayor Thomas claimed the vacated building was safe and even went so far as to invite the press or anyone else to come to the building and enjoy lunch with him. No one seriously considered his offer.

Officials from the Department of Nuclear Safety came to Ottawa in 1984 and after making a preliminary examination announced before a special city council meeting, the building that had been determined to radiate unsafe levels of radioactivity should be torn down.

The spokesman for the agency mentioned an amount the state would spend, but it did not cover the costs of finding an area to deposit the contaminated material. The state officials said $2.5 million would be used to remove the building and its contents.

*Former Site of Luminous Processes Building*
*Photo by Author*

In 1986 the State of Illinois spent $4,500 to demolish the building. It was determined that the surrounding soil and parts of the building including its foundations were highly contaminated. The workers who were hired to dismantle the building were required to wear color coded helmets and uniforms that would designate the area where they would work. The remnants of the building and the contaminated soil were carefully removed under strict supervision and transported by trucks to government controlled areas in Washington State.

The Luminous Processes Corporation was fined $30,000 for several health violations. There was an estimate of an additional $6.4 million to clean up those areas in and around Ottawa where the rubble from the old Radium Dial Company and the old Ottawa Township High School had been located and where much of the radioactive debris was dumped and then asphalted over.

Several privately owned residences were also identified as areas that would have to be examined for possible dangerous levels of radioactivity. Many home owners in Ottawa claimed their yards, sidewalks and driveways were torn up and soil samples were taken.

In the 1980's the U.S. Environmental Protective Agency established a "superfund" to clean up Ottawa and to excavate 14 areas that were determined to be "hot" and also to remove the contamination where landfill made up of the rubble from the old high school was dumped. Many felt the contamination had spread into the soil and ground water affecting residential and commercial properties around town. The danger of radium was no longer restricted to just those people who worked with radium or their worksites. There were more than a dozen sites that were located but there was still more work to be done.

When the funds ran out, many of the excavated areas were simply covered over until more money was available. There were still areas outside of Ottawa that needed to be excavated. It was estimated it would take at least five years to clean up at a cost of $80 million.

In August 2015, the U.S. Environmental Protection Agency returned to Ottawa to focus on an area identified as NPL-4-site an area on Canal Road just east of Ottawa where large amounts of radium had been dumped. Workers erected a chain link fence clearly marked "Dangerous Radioactive Materials" and to stay out, were operating heavy equipment to remove several tons of radium contaminated soil. Dust controls were also put in place to be used during digging and loading operations to make the area safe for those who lived near the site.

The Ottawa sites were added to the National Priorities (Superfund) list when in 1991 radium pollution was found in several areas in and around the city. The work to remove the contaminated soil in this area is still a work in progress. It was scheduled to be completed by December 2015 but there is still several tons of contaminated soil yet to be removed. The estimated cost for the entire clean up was $40 million. By the end of December, large amounts of contaminated soil were still being removed. Several huge plastic wrapped large squares of dirt remained stacked to be picked up by trucks to be transported to government designated facilities in the Northwest part of the U.S.

*Current Excavations on Canal Road in Ottawa.*
*Photo by Author*

The major positive note that came out of the actions taken by the dial painters and radium girls was a federal law known as the Occupational Safety and Health Act that requires all workplaces to be safe and gave workers the right to sue their employers over labor abuses and to eliminate personal injury and illnesses from the work place.

For several years, where Luminous Processes Inc. once stood is now a city parking lot.

# 17
# The Return of A Radium Girl to Ottawa

Recently, an 8th grader identified as Madeline Piller wrote a social studies project about the radium girls and wondered why some kind of a memorial had not been placed in Ottawa for them. She quietly but persistently lobbied the city officials for more than five years to have a memorial erected to honor those girls who had worked at Radium Dial and Luminous Processes and sacrificed their health and many who had given their lives.

Mayor Robert Eschbach agreed something should be done now that several books and a documentary entitled Radium City had been filmed. With financial backing from many of the local labor unions and many local businesses, Madeline's father who was a professional sculptor, designed and made a life size bronze statue of a radium dial girl holding a paint brush and a wilted tulip. The dying tulip symbolized death from the radioactive contamination of the dial worker girl. Perhaps it served as a symbol of a coal mine canary and the flower had wilted from the radioactive breath of the radium girl. The statue is surrounded by a beautiful landscaped area at the corner of the Fulton and Jefferson Streets where the entrance of the Luminous Processes Corporation once stood.

*Radium Girl Memorial*
*Photo by Author*

On September 2, 2011 which was Labor Day the dedication of the statue of the radium girl was presented before a large gathering of people. Some of the original dial painters were on hand to witness the dedication.

As Mayor Eschbach explained, people at that time did not want to talk much about the situation, and they really tried to sweep the incident under the rug. Now with the dedication of the "Radium Girl" statue and site, the subject of the dial painters no longer seem to be an off-limits topic of conversation.

There are still areas around the town that will have to be excavated but the city that had been accused of failing to see the light has for the most part become safe and the "Friendly City of Ottawa" has come to terms with the devastating period of the radium poisoning fear and is once again at peace with itself.

In researching the facts to put this book together, I have known several people in Ottawa who were affected by this tragedy that happened many decades ago.

One of my neighbors, Jeanne Wultzen, who worked at Luminous Processes Inc. for a short time before studying to become a nurse, died from osteoporosis that might have been caused by being exposed to radium. Her rib cage was severely honeycombed resulting in not being able to breathe. According to Jeanne's younger sister, Nancy Quinzio, she worked as a dial painter for just one summer while she was still attending school. She said that shortly before her sister's death, she came to her house to see Jeanne who was obviously in pain, although she said it was nothing to cause concern. Jeanne was taken to the hospital where it was learned she had five fractured vertebrae. She also said she had fractured her arm and it never seemed to heal correctly.

Mrs. Quinzio also mentioned in an interview that several women she knew who worked at Radium Dial or Luminous Processes Inc. suffered from the symptoms of cancer.

A former colleague of mine Joanne Schuster Fox who was employed for several years as a biology teacher and girls track coach at Marquette Academy, spent a lot of time at the Marquette athletic field in the late 1970's and early 1980's. I purchased her house in 1987 when she and her husband, Owen moved to the State of Oregon.

Soon after they left Ottawa, Joanne was diagnosed with cancer. She died a few years later at age 49. Several of her friends, including one who is a former colleague of mine, Linda Malley, felt sure Joanne had been unknowingly exposed to the radium that had been deposited near the Marquette athletic field.

Another colleague of mine who also taught biology grew up in a house located behind the old Ottawa Township High School, Maureen Wolfe told me her mother died several years later from cancer. She also said that almost every resident who lived within two blocks of her home had contracted some form of cancer and several died within a few years.

In the late 1990's I observed workers in white uniforms with filtered masks working less than two blocks from my home near the

Marquette athletic field. They worked for several months excavating and removing several tons of contaminated soil.

The cleanup of areas where radium-contaminated soil has been located continues to be a work in progress. The city that many said had failed to see the light has come to terms with a decade of several deaths and illnesses that left a scar across the history of Ottawa nearly a century ago, but the city is at peace with itself and continues in the 21st Century to grow and maintain its motto, "the Friendly City". The story of the Ottawa dial painting girls still needs to be told.

The End

# References Cited

Ottawa Scouting and Historical Museum
Ottawa, Illinois

Radium Girls Animation Project
Katie Todaro
2012

The Radium Watch Dial Painters
D.S. Butterworth
Lost Horse Press

Catherine Donohue Papers
Northwestern University

A Brief History of Standard Chemical Company
Joel O. Lubenan

Reddick Library
Ottawa, Illinois

Radium City Documentary
Carole Langer Productions 1987

Photos courtesy of
Mollie Perrot who shared several pictures from her personal collection to the Radium Dial display at the Ottawa Scouting and Historical Museum.

## Interviews with:

Wayne Wiesbrock
Caretaker: St. Columba Cemetery
Ottawa, Illinois

Nancy Quinzio
Sister of Jeanne Lane Wultzen

Linda Malley
Retired teacher
Marquette Academy

Maureen Wolfe
Retired Biology Teacher
Marquette Academy

Special thanks to
Kevin Bressendorf and staff
of Computer Spa
Ottawa, Illinois

Leslie Suppan
Ottawa, Illinois
for her help to prepare this manuscript for publication.

CPSIA information can be obtained
at www.ICGtesting.com
Printed in the USA
FFHW011802060919
54828230-60522FF

9 781478 768869